we love you...

£7.99

This is an independent publication.

It is completely unofficial and unauthorised and, as such, has no connection with the artist or artists featured, or with any organisation or individual connected in any way whatsoever with the artist or artists featured.

Any quotes within this publication which are attributed to the celebrity, or celebrities, featured have been sourced from other publications, or from the internet, and, as such, are a matter of public record. They have not been given directly to the author by the celebrity, or celebrities, themselves.

Whilst every effort has been made to ensure the accuracy of information within this publication, the publisher shall have no liability to any person or entity with respect to any inaccuracy, misleading information, loss or damage caused directly or indirectly by the information contained within this book.

ISBN: 978-1-907823-13-8

we love you... TAKE THAT

A Pillar Box Red Publication

Written by Martin Johnston
Designed by Jane Greig

CONTENTS

TAKE THAT – SUPER STAR FACT FILE

Take that are unquestionably one of the biggest boy bands of all time. With an exciting career full of ups and downs, musical differences and a string of hugely successful hits under their belt they have soared to super stardom, each member of the band having also carved out their own successful career on top of their success with the band.

MEMBERS: Gary Barlow, Howard Donald, Jason Orange, Mark Owen and Robbie Williams (if his return to the band can be classed as permanent)

BACKGROUND: The boys have enjoyed a long and varied career but where did it all begin? Here's the facts all Take That fans need to know!

☆ Take That were put together In 1989, by Nigel Martin-Smith. He first signed Gary Barlow and was so impressed with his song writing and musical skills that he built the band around him, holding auditions in Manchester in 1990.

☆ Howard used to work as a vehicle painter and managed to get time off to audition for the band. He was actually one of the oldest to audition but was chosen and subsequently became part of Take That's history! It was also Howard who recommended fellow street dancer Jason Orange who was also offered a place in the band.

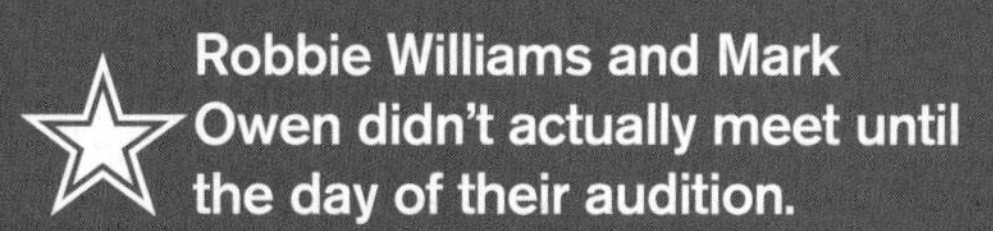

☆ Robbie Williams and Mark Owen didn't actually meet until the day of their audition.

☆ The band's breakthrough single was 'It only takes a minute' which reached number 7 in the UK singles chart. Not bad for a brand new group! 'Could it be Magic' did even better on its release peaking at number 3.

☆ The band's debut album, Take That and Party, was released in 1991 and was an instant success.

☆ Take That got their first number one single in 1993, 'Pray' which was from the 'Everything Changes' album.

In July 1995 Robbie Williams left Take That, although the band did continue to perform without him for a while.

13th February 1996 was the date that Take That announced to millions of heartbroken fans that they were splitting up as a band to work on solo material. At the time this was an absolutely huge event in the music world, receiving front page coverage across all the major newspapers.

It wasn't until 9th May 2006 after a 10-year absence from the music scene that Take That announced that they were returning to the music scene, signing with Polydor records in a reported £3million deal. Wow!

Their comeback album 'Beautiful World' entered the charts straight in at number 1 proving that the fans had definitely embraced Take That's return!

Not satisfied with being the most popular band on earth, they also began to start work on movie soundtracks, with the song "Rule the World" featured in the hit film 'Stardust' being one of their most popular!

The band have recently been reconciling with ex band-mate Robbie Williams who has appeared on tour with the boys once more. It is unclear as to whether he's officially back in the band at the moment, but things look promising with Gary saying "Robbie's return has been so well accepted by the fans" when talking about recent updates.

All of the members have branched out into different projects with Gary being the one most in the public eye the past couple of years. His most recent achievements were arranging a charity trip to Mount Kilimanjaro and becoming a judge on the 2011 series of the X Factor, exciting times!

we love you...

GARY BARLOW FUN FACTS

Let's fix the spotlight firmly on Gary Barlow as we list some of the coolest facts that you might not know about the most versatile and well-rounded Take That band member!

NAME: Gary Barlow
D.O.B: 20th January 1971
PLACE OF BIRTH: Frodsham, Cheshire

* **FACT 1** Gary is a rather youthful looking 40 year-old. He celebrated his 40th birthday this year in London for a special charity gig. Elton John was also present and apparently took to the stage to give a special birthday message. Oh to be a fly on the wall at that event!

* **FACT 2** When the group disbanded and Gary's solo album didn't do as well as he would have liked, he made the decision to give up singing for a whopping 7 years! We are glad he didn't give up completely though as Take That just wouldn't have been the same without him.

* **FACT 3** Gary has written some amazing tracks for other famous musicians including Charlotte Church and Dame Shirley Bassey.

* **FACT 4** Gary Barlow wasn't always on a pop star's wages, he once performed at the Connah's Quay Labour Club in the late eighties earning just £18 per performance on Saturday evenings. How things have changed!

* **FACT 5** Gary married one of his backing dancers from the 1995 'Nobody Else' tour and they now have three children together. See, who says that you should never mix businesses and pleasure? It certainly worked for Gary in this case.

MARK OWEN
FUN FACTS

NAME: Mark Anthony Patrick Owen
D.O.B: 27th January 1972
PLACE OF BIRTH: Oldham, Greater Manchester

* **FACT 1** Mark's debut single 'Child' reached number 3 in the singles chart. The super-catchy track 'Four Minute Warning' was also a top 5 hit.

* **FACT 2** Mark won the second series of Celebrity Big Brother in 2002. He gained a massive 75% of the votes as the British public once again fell in love with his laid-back attitude and good looks!

* **FACT 3** Mark won 'Most Fanciable Male' at the 'Smash Hits Poll Winners Party' three years in a row!

* **FACT 4** Although his solo career didn't always go exactly to plan, with some albums charting in low positions, as a solo artist, Mark Owen has sold over 400,000 records worldwide and 40 million with Take That.

* **FACT 5** Mark doesn't always get a chance to take centre stage in the band, but the songs that he has had solo performances on are: 'Babe' 'Shine' 'Up all Night' where his distinctly good voice always stands out amongst the others.

JASON ORANGE
FUN FACTS

NAME: Jason Thomas Orange
D.O.B: 10th July 1970
PLACE OF BIRTH: Manchester

* **FACT 1** Jason has fantastic breakdancing skills and was a member of the Manchester-based 'Street Machine' crew and appeared in the TV show 'The Hitman and Her' which gave him his first taste of fame at a young age, before the Take That days!

* **FACT 2** When Take That split, Jason was the only member of the band not to embark on a solo music career. Instead he decided to focus on shaping himself an acting career and as a result appeared in 'Killer Net' in 1998 on Channel 4 and stage production 'Gob' at the King's Head theatre in London.

* **FACT 3** Proving that he also has the brains to go with his talent and charm, Jason went to South Trafford College in Altrincham, studying psychology, biology, history and sciences at A-Level after Take That split.

* **FACT 4** Jason Orange has a twin brother called Justin and four other brothers as well as three half-sisters. Family is very important to him and always prioritises them before everything else.

* **FACT 5** Jason has yet to marry or settle down and enjoys the single life. Even back in 2007, the then 37 year old was quoted as saying, "I still feel too young to get married. I really want to, and I would love to have kids." "At the moment I like life the way it is and I don't want to do it just because I feel I have to while I'm young." So there's still hope yet, ladies!

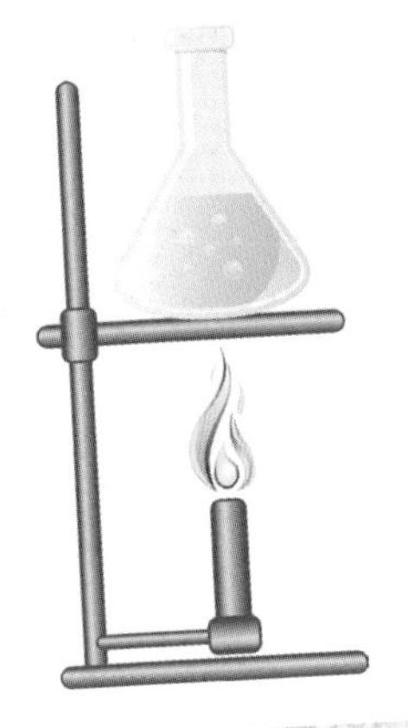

HOWARD DONALD FUN FACTS

NAME: Howard Donald
D.O.B: 28th April 1968
PLACE OF BIRTH: Manchester

* **FACT 1** Howard is a keen DJ with a big following, especially in Germany. He goes by the name 'DJ HD' and enjoys keeping up with this when not on tour with the Take That boys.

* **FACT 2** Howard suffered a collapsed lung on the 'Beautiful World' Tour in 2007, this was so severe that he had to remain on a hospital ward for two days whilst the other band members performed without him. Luckily he was well enough to make a much welcome return for the final leg of the tour, meaning that the band could perform the finale in true Take That style!

* **FACT 3** Howard is the proud father to two daughters named Grace and Lola, Grace being the older of the two girls.

* **FACT 4** Howard's solo numbers in Take That include: "If This is Love" "Never Forget" "Beautiful World" "Mancunian Way" "What is Love" "Here" "Affirmation" and "Aliens"

* **FACT 5** Howard turned his hand to playing the drums for several songs on the 'Progress' album. He can also play the piano and has dabbled in song writing. What a busy guy!

ROBBIE WILLIAMS FUN FACTS

NAME: Robert (Robbie) Peter Williams
D.O.B: 13th February 1974
PLACE OF BIRTH: Stoke-on-Trent, Staffordshire

* **FACT 1** Robbie has a scar on his head. It is reported that he got this from jumping into a fountain in Italy that turned out to have no water in it. Oopsey!

* **FACT 2** Robbie Williams has sold more than 57 million albums worldwide and is the best-selling male solo artist in the UK.

* **FACT 3** Robbie has a keen interest in the Paranormal. He believes in the existence of UFOs and extra-terrestrials and even took part in a documentary for TV talking about his belief in them and taking part in research trips and field searches. Spooky stuff!

* **FACT 4** Robbie is a keen footballer and enjoys taking part in charity football games, often alongside his best friend and fellow celeb Jonathan Wilkes. The two have a strong and often comedic friendship and have been friends for many years.

* **FACT 5** After a break from Take That and a fantastic solo career, Robbie and the boys finally put their differences aside and on 15th July 2010, Robbie announced he was returning to Take That. There has been a great reception from the fans with regards to his return and so far things seem to be going well, with Robbie taking slightly more of a back-seat role within the group, just enjoying being part of it all again.

we love you...

TAKE THAT QUOTES

Take That always have a lot to say, the guys are constantly being asked questions and giving their answers, opinions and thoughts to the media. Here are a few of the things there were quoted as saying.

Mark Owen talking to 'Time Out' about Robbie Williams: "It's great to see him perform with such passion. Because speaking to him a year and a half ago, you'd get the impression that he wouldn't do it. He thought he wouldn't be able to get on stage again. He'd fallen out of love with it all. The spark's back, he's bouncing around. We feel so blessed that he's back with us - it's such a joyful thing, "it really is."

Jason Orange talking about being compared to Robbie's success after the band split: "What did my head in, what really vexed me in the 10 years I had off, if I was on a beach somewhere

in Thailand, or at college – things I loved doing and chose to do – it was always going to be considered by other people as, 'Oh, he's taken a step down', Oh, he's a failure', while Robbie's up there, 'Look at what he's doing now.'"

Mark Owen whilst talking about the worry of trying to top the 'Circus' tour with Progress: "That's just it," says Owen. "How are we going to top the last one? That was the first question we had to ask when planning the Progress tour. The first and most important thing we did was to get the songs sorted and build the show around that. We have a lot of confidence in the set list we've built over 20 years. But us being us, we can't just go up and do that, we have to think, 'We could sing the song, but we could also do it while flying out of a plane. Come on!"

Howard speaking to GQ Mag: "I suppose I kind of look up to the other guys," says Howard. "I do hate myself sometimes for being the way I am. I always sit back in group interviews and wait for someone else to answer because in my head their answer's always going to be better than mine. I try to pick my moments but they're few and far between."

Robbie speaking about having calmed down his wild lifestyle: "I don't go out at all now," Williams nods. "The only time people get a photograph of me is at an airport or coming out of the dentist."

"Howard was Rob's favourite, after Mark. He looked up to Howard like you would a big brother. Me and Howard had left school and had jobs by the time it all started with Take That, but Robbie hadn't. Those little things mean a lot when you're sixteen years old."
JASON ORANGE

TAKE THAT WORDSEARCH

Can you find all of these Take That related words in our Take That themed wordsearch?

AMILLIONLOVESONGS
BARLOW
CIRCUS
EVERYTHINGCHANGES
HOWARD
NEVERFORGET
THE FLOOD
ORANGE
PRAY
PROGRESS
ROBBIE
RULETHEWORLD
TAKETHAT

A	P	P	N	R	R	H	O	W	A	R	D	K	K	W	F	S
M	N	R	R	Y	K	N	D	N	H	M	V	R	G	X	M	E
I	F	R	N	A	K	R	G	S	Q	H	N	N	M	F	W	G
L	J	M	D	K	Y	M	U	T	K	W	W	K	X	M	V	N
L	D	T	Z	L	G	C	G	W	D	R	O	B	B	I	E	A
I	N	J	B	T	R	K	Y	Q	X	T	N	C	N	N	L	H
O	X	M	T	I	X	O	F	X	H	G	K	N	W	M	Q	C
N	T	R	C	B	T	X	W	F	L	F	V	R	O	H	Q	G
L	K	A	R	V	L	N	K	E	K	X	G	W	L	S	K	N
O	M	T	K	G	K	M	Q	D	H	G	N	O	R	S	V	I
V	P	K	G	E	R	G	O	X	M	T	R	G	A	E	D	H
E	H	L	K	M	T	O	N	V	K	A	E	Z	B	R	L	T
S	D	D	X	N	L	H	R	V	N	G	M	L	K	G	C	Y
O	V	V	H	F	R	C	A	G	T	K	L	L	U	O	P	R
N	K	D	E	D	N	T	E	T	F	B	M	R	L	R	Z	E
G	T	H	K	N	R	N	C	K	T	G	J	Z	M	P	M	V
S	T	E	G	R	O	F	R	E	V	E	N	T	R	Q	D	E

Answers on Page 61

we love you...

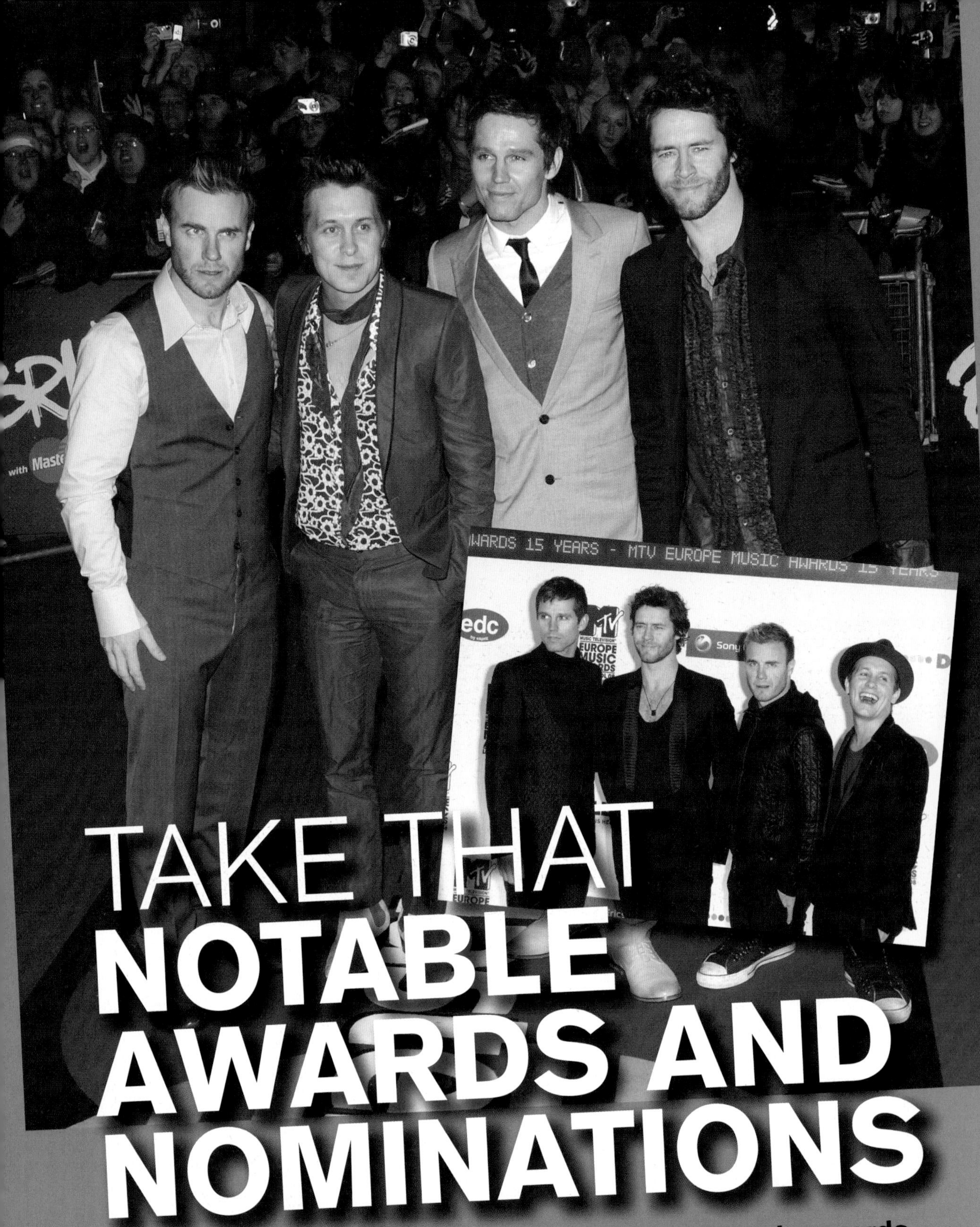

TAKE THAT NOTABLE AWARDS AND NOMINATIONS

Take That are one of the biggest winners of music awards the UK has ever known. Regularly seen sweeping the charts both back when they first got together and even now, years down the line!
They have proved to everyone that not only are they capable of performing sell-out shows and releasing chart-topping albums but that also, their talent is recognised by fans and industry insiders alike!

TAKE THAT NOTABLE AWARDS

2011
ARTIST : Take That Lyrics
BRITISH GROUP
BRIT Awards

2010
ARTIST : Take That Lyrics
Hall Of Fame
Q Music Awards

2008
SONG : Shine Lyrics
Best British Single
BRIT Awards

2008
ARTIST : Take That Lyrics
Best British Live Act
BRIT Awards

2007
SONG : Patience Lyrics
Best British Single
BRIT Awards

2006
ARTIST : Take That Lyrics
Q Idol Award
Q Music Awards

1996
SONG : Back For Good Lyrics
Best British Single
BRIT Awards

1995
ARTIST : Take That Lyrics
Best Live Act
MTV Europe Awards

1994
ARTIST : Take That Lyrics
Best Group
MTV Europe Awards

1994
SONG : Pray Lyrics
Best British Single
BRIT Awards

1994
SONG : Pray Lyrics
Best British Video
BRIT Awards

1993
SONG : Could It Be Magic Lyrics
Best British Single
BRIT Awards

TAKE THAT NOTABLE NOMINATIONS

2011
ALBUM : Progress Lyrics
BRITISH ALBUM OF THE YEAR
BRIT Awards

2010
SONG : Beatles Medley Lyrics
The BRITs Hits 30
BRIT Awards

2009
ARTIST : Take That Lyrics
Best Live Act
Q Music Awards

2009
ARTIST : Take That Lyrics
British Group
BRIT Awards

2008
ARTIST : Take That Lyrics
British Group
BRIT Awards

2008
ALBUM : Beautiful World Lyrics
Best British Album
BRIT Awards

TAKE THAT
STAR SIGNS

Have you ever wondered what Star Sign your favourite member of Take That is? We delve into the world of the Zodiac and horoscopes and see just how well the band's star signs correspond to their actual character traits and personalities!

The Aquarius Boys!

ROBBIE WILLIAMS
(13th February 1974):
Aquarius
MARK OWEN
(27th January 1972):
Aquarius
GARY BARLOW
(20th January 1971): Aquarius

Yes, strange as it may seem, three of the Take That boys are Aquarius. Robbie, Mark and Gary all share the same star sign!

About Aquarius
Lucky Day: Sunday and Saturday
Lucky Colour: Blue, Blue-green, Grey, Black
Positive Qualities: Truth-seeker, honest, probing, popular, amiable, broad-minded and creative. Sounds like the boys to us!
Aquarius Likes: fame and recognition, personal privacy, rainbows, dreams, magic, change for its own sake, eccentricity, surprises, and living within their means despite the many temptations which constantly surround them every waking moment.

Aquarians can often be categorized into two distinct types. The first type can be described as patient, gentle, sensitive and shy. While the second type (Robbie springs to mind here!) can be described as an exhibitionist, is livelier, exuberant and uses frivolity to conceal different aspects of their personality. In spite of their apparent differences, both types still possess strong wills and firm beliefs in their convictions.

Symbol: The Water Bearer
Ruling Planet: Uranus
Quality: Fixed
Element: Air
Closest Metal: Aluminium and Uranium
Lucky Gems: Aquamarine
Lucky Flowers: Orchids

Strengths

- Friendly and affable
- Intelligent
- Kind and compassionate
- Practical

Some other famous Aquarius people are: Jennifer Aniston, Joseph Gordon-Levitt, Ashton Kutcher, Taylor Lautner, Christina Ricci, John Travolta and Oprah Winfrey. They are definitely in good company!

Not all of the boys are Aquarius though, read on below for Jason and Howard's star signs!

JASON ORANGE: **Star Sign Cancer**
Jason was born on10th July 1970 making his star sign 'Cancer'

Character Traits

- Conservative and home-loving
- Seeks security
- Wise
- Hard worker

Likes

- Hobbies
- Romance
- Children
- Home and Country
- Parties

The colour for Cancer is Silver.

Lucky Day: Monday, Thursday
Lucky Colour: Orange, White
Symbol: The Crab
Ruling Planet: Moon
Quality: Cardinal
Element: Water
Closest Metal: Silver

Famous Fellow Cancarians:
Camilla Parker-Bowles, David Hasselhoff, George Michael, Harrison Ford, Jessica Simpson, Josh Hartnett, Kevin Bacon, Michael Phelps, Richard Branson, Tom Hanks, Tom Cruise.

Last but not least we have HOWARD DONALD, Howard's **star sign is Taurus.**

Taurus Character Traits:
Lucky Day: Friday, Monday
Lucky Colour: Blue, Blue-Green

Dependable, patient, persistent, and downright determined. Whenever he starts some work, no matter what it may be, he makes a point to see it through. He has a strong sense of tradition, is loyal to his family and friends, stable in nature, emotional, and very sentimental about his loved ones.

Among other Taurus characteristics, he values honour and integrity above all. His gentle and tolerant behaviour attracts people towards him. Taurus people often have good common sense and financial sense.

Symbol: The Bull
Ruling Planet: Venus
Quality: Fixed
Element: Earth
Closest Metal: Copper

Other Famous Taurus people include: Jessica Alba, Pierce Brosnan, Renee Zellweger, Stevie Wonder, Megan Fox, David Beckham, Tony Blair, Queen Elizabeth II.

GARY BARLOW AND THE X FACTOR

Gary Barlow is a multi-talented music legend as far as we're concerned. Not only has he achieved huge success both with Take That and on his solo albums, he's also an amazing song writer and all round talented guy!

It comes as no surprise that the X Factor signed him up as one of the judges for 2011 with TV insiders agreeing that he could bring a whole new dimension to the already popular show. Move over Simon Cowell, Mr Gary Barlow is in the house!

Gary has spoken out about his role on the show to various newspapers and in interviews and has a great enthusiasm for his role, he knows that he has the experience to deliver advice as a great mentor and we all know that he definitely has the talent to back up his opinions. He has a keen musical ear and can spot a potential star a mile off.

Speaking to the Daily Mirror about the X Factor Barlow says, "I want to

see all the talent come through the door. What's going to lift us is when someone comes on stage and makes our hairs stand up."

He also admitted that he was sad that his pal Cheryl Cole was not going to be a part of the 2011 X Factor as originally planned. He said, "I sent Cheryl some texts just saying 'Sending support'. She's a good friend of mine. I'm disappointed she's gone."
Gary couldn't wait to get on with the show though, and wanted to be part of every audition, desperate not to miss any of the potential talent that could walk through the door.

He was also excited about working with the rest of the judges, saying, "The other two girls are going to be great." Adding: "I love Tulisa - I've worked with N-Dubz before and I love working with them. She's great and is going to bring a whole new dimension to the show."

Gary is no stranger to hard work and hit the task of judging the X Factor and doing the 'Progress' tour with the rest of the band head on. It was no easy feat managing the two at the same time but he loves it and doesn't mind being kept busy. What a trooper!

we love you...

CROSSWORD

ACROSS

4 This band mate had to take time off from a car spraying plant to audition for Take That (6)

6 The song "Could It Be Magic' was originally a hit in the '70s for Barry_________ (7)

9 "How deep is your love" was originally a song for the Bee ______ (4)

10 The song "Rule The World" featured in this film (8)

13 Jason's surname (6)

16 The title of Gary Barlow's first autobiography (2,4)

17 Band mate who won rear of the year in 1997 (4,6)

18 Gary had his Madame Tussauds wax work melted down in favour of this female US pop star (7,6)

19 City where the band was formed (10)

20 Band mate who used to own a pet iguana called "Nirvana" (4,4)

DOWN

1 The name Howard is known as when he DJ's (2,2)

2 Gary will be a judge on this year's talent trek (1, 6)

3 Featured on "Relight My Fire'" (4)

5 Howard's energetic dancing caused him to have a collapsed______ (4)

7 The location of Take That's final performance before splitting up in 1996 (9)

8 The name of Howard and Jason's break dancing group (10)

11 Which original member of the band left in 1996 to pursue a solo career (6)

12 Which song features the lyrics "got your lipstick marks still on your coffee cup" (4,3,4)

14 The band's first UK number one (4)

15 Prestigious song writing award won by Take That for "Shine" (4,7)

Answers on Page 61

TAKE THAT CHARITY WORK

Take That are well known for their contributions to charities and charity related events. With Gary Barlow being one of the most well-known for doing incredibly good work in the charity world, it is great to see a successful band like these boys using their own fame and fortune to help others.

Some of the most notable things that we have seen Take That involved with for charity are below. Of course, there are many more things in the pipeline we're sure as the boys never really stop!

2009 Gary Barlow led a team of top celebrities up a tough mountain climb. The group made it to the top and raised an astounding £3.5 million for Comic Relief. Now that's what you call determination!

2010 In August 2010 Robbie Williams headlined at the 'Help the Heroes' concert, a fantastic charity who provide much needed support for injured soldiers.

2010 Take That performed together live on stage for Children in Need. The band sang their classic hit Never Forget live for the first time since Robbie Williams re-joined the group during their stellar performance at the BBC's star-studded charity night.

2011 Mark Owen donated x10 VIP tickets to their sold out 'Progress' tour to be auctioned in a kind gesture to help raise funds for 'Rainbow School' a school for children with autism, located not far from Mark's home. He said "Rainbow School was, unbeknown to me, literally only yards away from my front door and so after taking a tour of the school, meeting the children and its founder Karen, I decided that I'd really like to help in whatever way possible to support these amazing people."

2011 May 2011 saw Robbie Williams, Gary Barlow and Robin Gibb donating their time to perform at the 'Butterfly Benefit' fundraising event in aid of national charity, Caudwell Children. Robbie Williams became an official Ambassador for the Midlands-based children's charity last year and agreed to perform for the 250 invited guests ahead of Take That's record-breaking Progress Tour, which started two weeks later.

we love you...

TAKE THAT AND THEIR FAMOUS FRIENDS

Take That are a well respected band in the music industry today, with a lot of friends in high places! They are often spotted at the most star-studded events and most people would just love to get hold of their bulging contact book, if only for a few hours!

Take a look at just a few of the celebrities below who can proudly call themselves a friend of the one and only, Take That!

Cheryl Cole

Cheryl and Gary have been good friends for years. She was invited to a Bingo themed bash at his house, in celebration of his wedding anniversary along with her now ex-husband Ashley Cole. Gary and the band have also been in touch with Cheryl recently when it was revealed that she was no longer working alongside Gary on The X Factor 2011.

Fearne Cotton

This Radio 1 DJ is a firm friend of Gary Barlow and an old pal of the boys from their Take That days. She struck up a particularly strong bond with Gary when the two climbed Mount Kilimanjaro together for Comic Relief and the two have remained in touch since then.

Kylie Minogue

Kylie sang with Robbie Williams on his hit single "Kids" and is a good friend to both him and the Take That guys. It's always good to have the pint-sized pop princess in your contact list!

Lulu

Lulu first collaborated with Take That on their hit single "Re-light My Fire" which was an instant success with fans. She toured with the boys and still keeps in contact with them all on a regular basis.

Ellie Goulding

British singer song-writer Ellie Goulding performed at Gary Barlow's 40th birthday bash in 2011. She took to the stage to duet with Gary after the two made contact and hit it off previously to that. Ellie is young and talented and has a great respect for the Take That boys.

Nicole Kidman

This super successful flame-haired Australian actress has also gained some singing experience over the last few years of her career. With her appearance in the movie Moulin Rouge requiring her to challenge her vocal chords she also took to the music scene with our very own Robbie Williams in his hit single 'Something Stupid' which became Robbie's first Christmas Number 1 single in 2001.

TAKE THAT AND MOVIE SOUNDTRACKS

Take That have now become so successful that they are being asked to work on soundtracks for the hottest movies worldwide. Do you know your Take That movie and music trivia? Below are some of the coolest movies that the boys have provided songs for and the lowdown on their aspirations for future projects.

X-MEN: FIRST CLASS

This hit movie sequel charts the epic beginning of the X-Men saga, and reveals a secret history of famous global events. Before mutants had revealed themselves to the world, and before Charles Xavier and Erik Lensherr took the names Professor X and Magneto, they were two young men discovering their powers for the first time. Take That were asked to appear on the official movie soundtrack and they chose the catchy track 'Love, Love' with some very relevant lyrics and a hi-tech sound, it fits right in!

STARDUST

One of Take That's most well-known movie tracks has to be 'Rule the World' from the Stardust soundtrack. "Rule the World" is the first song written by Take That specifically for a film.

"Stardust," based on the best-selling graphic novel by Neil Gaiman and Charles Vess, takes audiences on an adventure that begins in a village in England and ends up in places that exist in an imaginary world. A young man named Tristan (Charlie Cox) tries to win the heart of Victoria (Sienna Miller), the beautiful but cold object of his desire, by going on a quest to retrieve a fallen star.

Fans fell in love with Take That's amazing single and it peaked at

number 2 in the charts, being held off only by Leona Lewis's super hit 'Bleeding Love'.

BOND, JAMES BOND!

Take That would love to do a James Bond theme tune. Jason says: "If we were asked we'd be flipping all over it!" (from GQ). Take That fans in fact did a petition for them to do the Quantum of Solace theme tune. Here's hoping that this might not be far off for the boys as we know they would do the movie justice with one of their fab songs!

'WHEN WE WERE YOUNG' - THE THREE MUSKETEERS

Gary Barlow, Howard Donald, Jason Orange, Mark Owen and Robbie Williams were inspired to write the ballad after a private screening of the film in Los Angeles with the film's director Paul W.S. Anderson. When asked about the new single Gary said: "The film is visually so rich and beautiful that our main challenge was to then match it musically. We've returned to guitars, real pianos and a conventional song structure to achieve this. We also thought that the Musketeers reminded us of ourselves."

FAVOURITE SOUNDTRACKS

All of Take That are huge movie fans themselves. Howard's favourite soundtrack is for the film Tron, starring Jeff Bridges. Jason thinks that the soundtrack for the film Hanna by the Chemical Brothers should be good. Lots of the Take That guys also have kids so we can imagine there being lots of Disney and musical-themed cartoons around the house as well!

We are sure that this is only the beginning of a very long line of movie themes for Take That!

we love you...

TAKE THAT
2011 PROGRESS TOUR

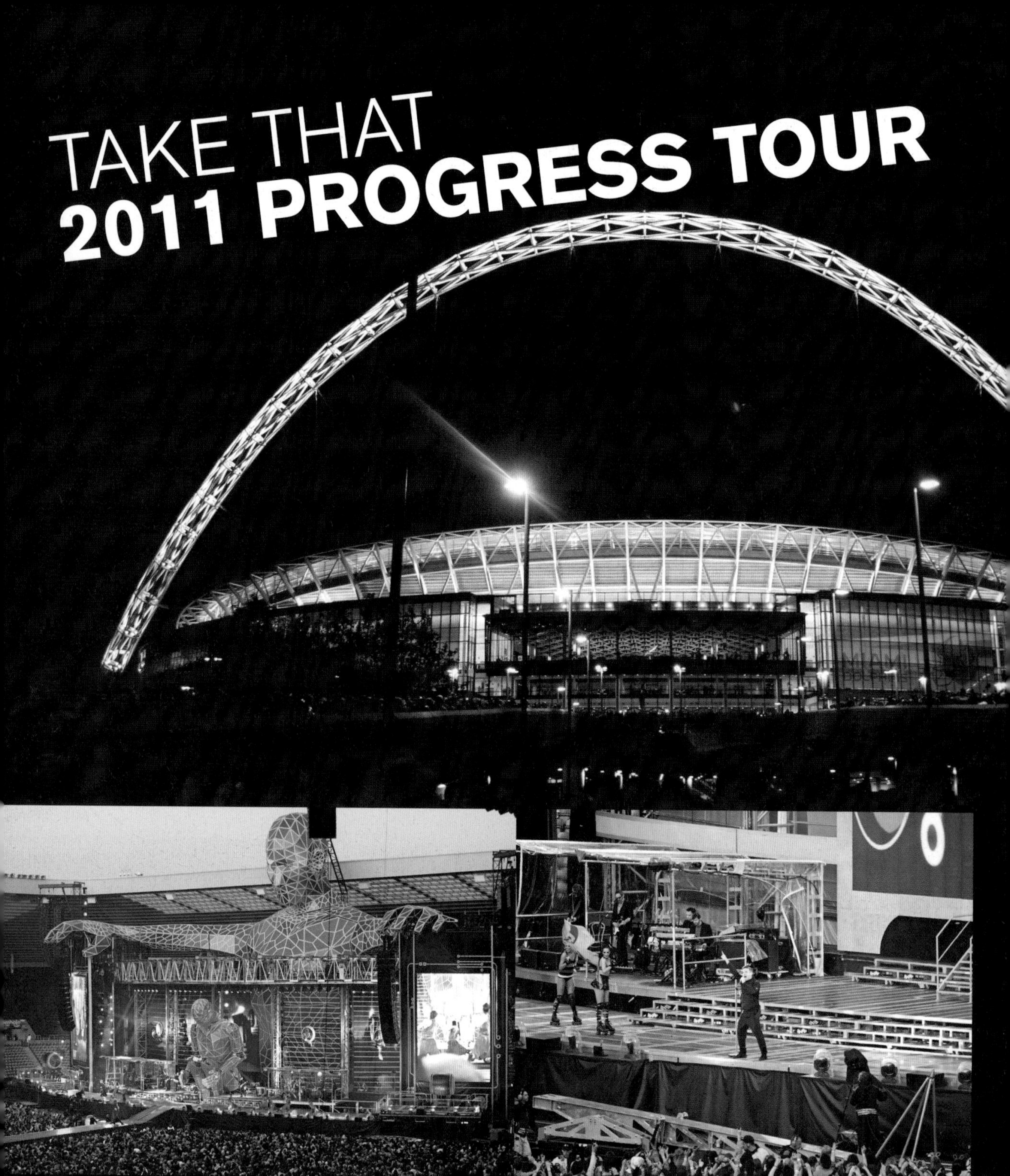

The 2011 'Progress' tour and album of the same name has been a real labour of love for the guys of Take That, each of them fearing that it wasn't going to live up to the amazing spectacle of the previous 'Circus' tour which had created an overwhelming buzz with fans.

The Progress Tour was the first time that the fab five had shared the stage together in an unbelievable 15 years and an apprehensive Mark was quoted as saying "We just wanted a tour that did justice to the reunion, to Robbie playing with us again."

They needn't have worried though; as the lads have done themselves proud with the latest tour, proving that they really are 'back for good' and delivering sights and sounds that

wow the crowds time and time again. They even had The Pet Shop Boys supporting, to keep the upbeat mood going strong.

With 'Progress' the album being the fastest selling album in the UK this century and having sold more than 2 million copies in the UK already, we think that Take That have certainly gone above and beyond everyone's expectations!

PROGRESS TOUR FACT AND FIGURES

- There were 36 dates on the Progress tour – 27 of which are in the UK.
- In total, 1.76m people in the UK and Ireland saw Gary, Mark, Howard, Jason and Robbie perform live last summer. That makes it officially the biggest tour in UK and Irish music history.
- The guys played a record-breaking eight nights at London's Wembley Stadium, making them the only act ever to play eight dates at the stadium, overtaking the previous record held by Michael Jackson who played seven nights on his 1988 Bad World Tour.
- There was a team of 287 people on the road with Progress Live with an extra 160 local crew in each city.
- The stage was 60m wide and 30m high.
- 104 trucks transported the production round the UK and Europe.
- From an empty stadium, it takes 48 hours to build the stage and set; and from when the band walk off stage, it takes 19 hours to take it all down again.
- 22 tonnes of electrical cabling were used, measuring 18km in total.
- At each date, a field kitchen was set up where 14 chefs and catering staff prepared more than 1100 restaurant-quality meals per day.
- Take That had five costume changes throughout the show and their 31 performers had nine.
- The huge robot in the show has been given the nickname of Om. He is 20m high and weighs 25 tons. It took 14 weeks to build him.
- Half of the stage the band used on their upcoming tour was made in the USA, while the other half was made in the UK.

ROBBIE WILLIAMS - THE WANDERER RETURNS!

Robbie Williams history in Take That has been one made up from many ups and downs. The band have had their fair share of differences but despite Robbie leaving the band in 1995 it was later announced in July 2010 that Robbie would record again with Take That as a five piece for the first time in 15 years!

ROBBIE'S RETURN - TAKE THAT QUOTES

The rest of the band all had things to say about Robbie's return to Take That, here are a few of the best quotes about Robbie's return!

Jason Orange said it was "absolutely brilliant," adding, "I'm over the moon that Robbie's back with us, however long it lasts. I just want to enjoy our time with him. Life is beautifully strange sometimes." We couldn't have put it better ourselves, Jason!

Robbie was quoted as saying he was "embarrassingly excited" and reuniting with his former group felt like "coming home" while band mate Mark Owen added that it "feels like a dream".

Mark Owen also said at the time: "Getting the five of us to be in a room together, although always a dream, never actually seemed like becoming a reality.

"Now the reality of the five of us making a record together feels like a dream. It's been an absolute delight spending time with Rob again. But I'm still a better footballer."

"Twenty years in the making, 15 years in the waiting, five years deliberating," he declared. "Ladies and gentlemen – the Take That show." As Robbie stepped out on stage to perform with the band again.

This became huge news in the media world, with everyone quick to ask if Robbie really was "Back for Good" or if it was just a passing brief appearance with the band. Some fans were wary at first but when the boys' obvious enthusiasm to be back together again started to shine through in interviews the general opinion was that of support and acceptance for Robbie.

At the time Gary praised the fans for their continued support saying "Robbie's return has been so well accepted by the fans" clearly being proud at what the group had achieved so many years later.

Robbie still has plans to work on solo material and it isn't clear if he will always remain a Take That member. It is definitely great to see how well things are progressing though and things look good for the future, especially with Gary also lending a hand to his friend's music wherever he can. It does look as if the turbulent times of Take That and Robbie Williams may be water under the bridge at long last.

Take That, combined with the solo sales of Robbie Williams, have sold more than 80 million albums. They've had 14 number one albums, 18 number one singles, played to more than 14.5 million people live, won 20 Brit Awards, eight MTV Awards and five Ivor Novellos. That sounds pretty impressive to us!

we love you...

SPOT THE **DIFFERENCE**

Take a look at the pictures below. There are six subtle differences between the two. Are you enough of an eagle eyed Take That fan to spot all of the differences? Have a go and check your answers on Page 61 to see how well you did.

TAKE THAT STYLE SECRETS

Take That are one of the most stylish boy bands of all time! Their look has constantly changed and evolved with them as they have made the transition from young, fresh boy band to mature, stylish performers. We love Take That for their amazing personalities and their equally well matched sense of style. Here is all of the hot gossip and info on the Take That style secrets of past and present!

Take That's style has changed a lot over the last 10 years. We have seen the boys go from bright, fun and young clothing to a style that is perfectly in tune with them and with their individual personalities and definitely a lot more grown up.

Take That's stylist, Luke Day, arguably the most influential figure in menswear right now, told the Guardian newspaper: "Since I've been working with the group, I don't think we've ever done anything that's involved sunshine," he says. "Winter is just better for older guys. And generally speaking, I don't think colours work too well on men either. Dark tones make them seem more serious and an older guy always looks good in a big coat, fur and scarves."

Making Take That look good, says Day, isn't hard, now that they're happy with their constantly evolving wardrobes.

Gary's dress sense is probably the most conservative of the group, with him preferring a simple look that doesn't go over the top and is casual yet stylish. Gary's style tends to reflect his personality and makes him seem approachable yet still on trend.

Reports are that some of Mark Owen's favourite brands are 'Lanvin' 'Dries Van Noten' and Gucci.

Howard is happy to wear cropped, carrot-shaped strides from Top Man or John Vavartos depending on his mood. A bit of a change from the old Take That days!

Robbie really likes 'Lobb of St James's' a bespoke cobbler to the royal family none the less.

Nothing like stepping out in style, hey Rob! Whilst he is still the most daring of the group with his dress sense even Robbie has toned down the flashy jewellery and accessories that he was previously well known for and adopted a calmer, fresher look that seems to fit with the band's new attitude as a whole.

It is without question that Take That's latest look is really working for them and they look better and happier than ever in their own skin. Let's look forward to many more new and exciting styles from the boys as they continue their long and winding career path.

TAKE THAT LYRICS QUIZ

How well do you know your Take That lyrics? Can you spot the odd one out below? You can find the answers at the back to see if you were right!

A A million love songs later, and here I am trying to tell you that I care. A million love songs later and here I am.

B Oh written in the stars, a million miles away, a message to the main, Ooooh, seasons come and go, but I will never change, and I'm on my way

C Whatever I said, whatever I did, I didn't mean it, I just want you back for good, want you back, want you back, I want you back for good.

D All I do each night is pray, Hoping that I'll be a part of you again someday, all I do each night is think, of all the times I close the door to keep my love within.

E You, you're such a big star to me, you're everything I wanna be, but you're stuck in a hole, and I want you to get out.

Answers on Page 61

COLOURING IN

TAKE THAT
A LOOK TO THE FUTURE

So, we all now know what Take That are up to lately, what they have done in the past and what we think makes them so great but what might our favourite boy band be up to next year, or the year after that? In this section we take a look at Take That's future plans and things that the boys aim to accomplish.

TAKE THAT FUTURE PLANS

Take That have a lot of things coming up for the next year or two. They are the kind of band who always have something new in the pipeline but here are just a few little snippets of gossip for you about what you can expect to see from them in the not so distant future...

X FACTOR 2011

Gary is of one of the judges on The X Factor 2011. This is a great career move for him and he is not only a fantastic musician but a fair and honest person so we think he will be just perfect for the role. Who knows what talent Gary Barlow may uncover in his determined and exciting talent search?

ROBBIE FLIES SOLO

Ok, he may be back with the band but we all know that Robbie likes the freedom of being able to work on his solo singles and projects at the same time. He will have a new single out soon and Gary Barlow is also reportedly going to produce Robbie's next solo album for him, according to recent reports.

FUTURE NEWS ROUNDUP!

Ever the charity man, Gary Barlow will be performing on Children in Need in November, we are sure he will do himself and the charity proud as always!

In 2012, Gary will be the musical director for the Queen's Diamond Jubilee gig. A huge responsibility and a much speculated, high profile event.

Howard will be learning to fly. He will be taking on his private pilot's licence. He ordered a plane last year that will hopefully arrive in 2013. It is an amphibious plane so it can land on water and land. What a daredevil!

We are sure that there is much more to come from Take That but you will just have to wait to find out exactly what! We can't wait to see what they are up to during the next few years; whatever they do they will do it in style that's for SURE!

we love you...

TAKE THAT DISCOGRAPHY

ALBUMS

Take That And Party - 1992
Everything Changes - 1993
Nobody Else – 1995
Beautiful World – 2006
The Circus – 2008
Progress – 2010
Live Albums
The Greatest Day – Take That Present: The Circus Live – 2009
Compilation Albums
Greatest Hits – 1996
The Best Of Take That – 2001
Forever… Greatest Hits – 2002
Never Forget – The Ultimate Collection

EP's

Progressed – 2011

SINGLES

Do What You Like – 1991
Promises – 1991
Once You've Tasted Love – 1992
It Only Takes A Minute – 1992
I Found Heaven – 1992
A Million Love Songs – 1992
Could It Be Magic – 1992
Why Can't I Wake Up With You – 1993
Pray – 1993
Relight My Fire – 1993
Babe – 1993
Everything Changes – 1994
Love Aint Here Anymore – 1994
Sure – 1994
Back For Good – 1995
Never Forget – 1995
How Deep Is Your Love – 1996
Patience – 2006
Shine – 2007
I'd Wait For Life – 2007
Reach Out – 2007
Rule The World – 2007
Greatest Day – 2008
Up All Night – 2009
The Garden – 2009
Said It All – 2009
The Flood – 2010
Kidz – 2011
Love Love – 2011
When We Were Young - 2011

GEM &
BEX

TAKE THAT AND THEIR FANS

Take That have some of the most loyal and varied fans from around the world. They have fans who have followed them from day one when the band was first formed but they have also gathered a new generation of fans since re-forming recently.

Take That love their fans and are always singing their praises. The fans have also been notoriously supportive of the band in its various forms both with and without Robbie. Gary recently said "Rob's return has been so well accepted by the fans." "Even when we came back in 2005, the goal was to get us all back together eventually, but the fact that's actually worked out that way is incredible."

Take a look below for some of the key reasons that we think Take That's fans love them so much!

- Take That are a band who can appeal to anyone and everyone.
- Take That's music is upbeat and varied with songs to suit every mood!
- There is no age limit with Take That, they appeal to the young and the older generations and cater for both with their music.
- Each Take That band member is different and they all have their own cheeky personalities and character traits.
- Take That are stylish and on trend, they know what works for them after years of being professionally photographed.
- Take That seem to care about their fans and always speak out about how much their support is appreciated.
- Take That have managed to successfully launch themselves back into today's competitive pop scene without a hitch, they obviously know what their fans want!
- Take That are the ultimate live act. Their stage tours are widely renowned and fans love them so much that some attend more than one night in a row. They must be doing something right!

we love you...

QUIZ **ANSWERS**

SPOT THE DIFFERENCE (PAGE 47)

WORDSEARCH (PAGE 22)

A	P	P	N	R	R	H	O	W	A	R	D	K	K	W	F	S
M	N	R	R	Y	K	N	D	N	H	M	V	R	G	X	M	E
I	F	R	N	A	K	R	G	S	Q	H	N	N	M	F	W	G
L	J	M	D	K	Y	M	U	T	K	W	W	K	X	M	V	N
L	D	T	Z	L	G	C	G	W	D	R	O	B	B	I	E	A
I	N	J	B	T	R	K	Y	Q	X	T	N	C	N	N	L	H
O	X	M	T	I	X	O	F	X	H	G	K	N	W	M	Q	C
N	T	R	C	B	T	X	W	F	L	F	V	R	O	H	Q	G
L	K	A	R	V	L	N	K	E	K	X	G	W	L	S	K	N
O	M	T	K	G	K	M	Q	D	H	G	N	O	R	S	V	I
V	P	K	G	E	R	G	O	X	M	T	R	G	A	E	D	H
E	H	L	K	M	T	O	N	V	K	A	E	Z	B	R	L	T
S	D	D	X	N	L	H	R	V	N	G	M	L	K	G	C	Y
O	V	V	H	F	R	C	A	G	T	K	L	L	U	O	P	R
N	K	D	E	D	N	T	E	T	F	B	M	R	L	R	Z	E
G	T	H	K	N	R	N	C	K	T	G	J	Z	M	P	M	V
S	T	E	G	R	O	F	R	E	V	E	N	T	R	Q	D	E

CROSSWORD (PAGE 33)

Accross

4) HOWARD
6) MANILOW
9) GEES
10) STARDUST
13) ORANGE
16)MYTAKE
17)GARYBARLOW
18) BRITNEYSPEARS
19) MANCHESTER
20) MARKOWEN

Down

1) DJHD
2) XFACTOR
3) LULU
5) LUNG
7) AMSTERDAM
8) STREETBEET
11) ROBBIE
12) BACK FOR GOOD
14) PRAY
15) IVOR NOVELLO

LYRICS QUIZ (PAGE 50)

Answer B is the odd one out

Photo: Tonis Valing / Shutterstock.com